GREAT SPORTING DATES

Keith West

OXFORD
UNIVERSITY PRESS

OXFORD
UNIVERSITY PRESS

Great Clarendon Street, Oxford OX2 6DP

Oxford University Press is a department of the University of Oxford.
It furthers the University's objective of excellence in research,
scholarship, and education by publishing worldwide in

Oxford New York

Auckland Bangkok Buenos Aires Cape Town Chennai
Dar es Salaam Delhi Hong Kong Istanbul Karachi Kolkata
Kuala Lumpur Madrid Melbourne Mexico City Mumbai
Nairobi São Paulo Shanghai Taipei Tokyo Toronto

Oxford is a registered trade mark of Oxford University Press
in the UK and in certain other countries

British Library Cataloguing in Publication Data

Data available

ISBN 0 19 917460 1

10 9 8 7 6 5 4 3 2

Also available in packs
Sports and Leisure Inspection Pack (one of each book) ISBN 0 19 917464 4
Sports and Leisure Class Pack (six of each book) ISBN 0 19 917465 2

www.oup.com/uk/primary

Printed in China

Acknowledgements

The Publisher would like to thank the following for their permission to reproduce photographs:
p 1 Hulton Archive; p 4 Empics/Tony Marshall; p 5 Hulton Arhive (top left, bottom left and right);
Allsport/Adrian Murrell (top right); p 6/7 Corbis/Reuters News Media (left), Empics/Jon Buckle (top
centre), Hulton Archive (right), Corbis/Tempsport (bottom centre); p 8 Allsport/Hulton Archive
(top), Empics/Topham Picturepoint (bottom); p 9 Allsport/Hulton Archive; p 10 Hulton Archive
(top), Empics/Topham Picturepoint (bottom); p 11 Empics/Topham Picturepoint (top and bottom);
p 12 Allsport (top), Empics/Alpha (bottom); p 13 Colorsport; p 14 Corbis/Bettmann (top),
Allsport/Tony Duffy (bottom); p 15 Empics/ S&G (top and bottom); p 16 Hulton Archive; p 17
Corbis/Roger Garwood and Trish Ainslie (top and bottom); p 18 Allsport/Steve Powell. (left),
Allsport/Tony Duffy (right); p 19 Hulton Archive (top), Allsport/Bob Martin (bottom); p 20 Allsport
(right), Empics/Jon Buckle (left); p 21 Empics/Ross Kinnaird (top and bottom); p 22 Empics/Neal
Simpson (left), Allsport (right); p 23 Corbis/S Carmona; p 24 Empics/Neal Simpson; p 25 Allsport
(both); p 26 Empics/Jon Buckle; p 27 Allsport; p 28 Corbis/Agence France Presse; p 29 Empics/Neal
Simpson (both); p 30 Empics/Neal Simpson (both);

Front cover photograph by CorbisDimitri Lundt
Back cover by Allsport/Hulton Archive

Contents

Introduction

Sport has certainly altered over the past hundred years. It used to be just a way people tried to get a bit of exercise and fill their leisure time after school or work. Nowadays, it is "big business". Sport sells newspapers. Television stations offer a lot of money for the rights to cover events such as Wimbledon or the FA Cup Final.

Competing at sports is now a full-time career for **professional** sportsmen and women. The best ones usually start serious training at a very young age, but an active career in sport is often a short one, and they retire early. However, some of them earn a great deal of money while they are "at the top".

▲ Michael Johnson – the only man to win both the 200 and 400 metres at both the World Championships and the Olympics

The Olympic Games

Sport has changed since the year 1900 when the second modern Olympic Games were held in Paris. People thought that event was a shambles! The discus champion, Robert Garrett from the USA, scattered a crowd he considered too close by throwing the discus into their midst. Swimmers had to struggle against strong currents in the River Seine, and marathon runners from other countries were held up by French supporters who wanted their hero to win. In the 1904 Olympics in St Louis, USA, an American, Fred Lorz, claimed victory in the marathon. Just as he was about to receive his award, the judges learned that he had hitched a lift from a passing car! Compare this with the high standards of performance at the Sydney Olympics in 2000.

4

Superheroes

▲ CB Fry practising at the wicket in 1905

Ian Botham playing football ▶
for Scunthorpe United

Who were the superheroes in the early days? In 1902, CB Fry was in the losing side of the FA Cup Final. He played for Southampton, who were beaten 1 – 0. Two days later he batted for a victorious London County cricket team. The only recent person to play for both a cricket team and a football team was Ian Botham, who was made England Cricket captain in 1980.

Motor racing

The first motor-racing Grand Prix took place in 1906 at Le Mans, France, and was won by the Hungarian driver Ferenc Szisz in a Renault. Stones on the track were a serious obstacle and the racing cars were taken down to the track by horses! Drivers needed to take their own supplies of spare petrol with them.

If the racing cars broke down, there were no pit stops. The drivers were responsible for their own repairs. What would modern racing drivers think of that?

Ferenc Szisz won ▶
the 1906 Grand
Prix in France...

◀ Felice Nazzaro came second, in a Fiat.

A century of sport

Many well-known sporting events started about 100 years ago. The first football match to be filmed was the FA Cup Final in 1901. The baseball World Series, the Tour de France cycling races and the Professional Golfer's Association championships all began before 1914, when the First World War interrupted many of the annual events.

▲ Serena and Venus Williams on their way to victory over Natalie Zvereva and Anna Kournikova in the Ladies' Doubles finals at Wimbledon in 2000

▼ Ellen McArthur in her yacht *Kingfisher*. She overcame tremendous difficulties to come second in the Vendée Globe round-the-world solo yacht race in 2001.

Sports kit

Modern technology and the invention of new materials have led to the development of all sorts of new sports equipment. These range from hi-tech clothing and footwear, to carbon-fibre tennis rackets and skis, as well as advanced electronic navigation equipment for yachts.

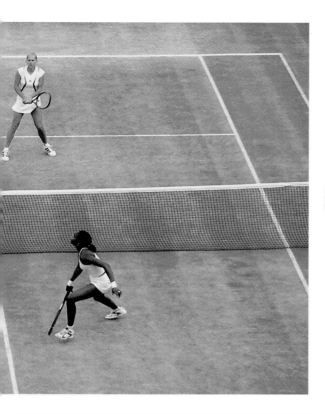

▲ Suzanne Lenglen at Wimbledon in 1922

When the French champion, Suzanne Lenglen, won Wimbledon in 1919 and 1920, people felt it was partly due to the fact that she wore clothes more suited to the game, rather than the long, flowing dresses and tight corsets that all ladies were expected to wear then. Top tennis stars today have the latest carbon-fibre rackets and specially designed clothing to help them perform at their very best.

Making sporting history

What will sport hold for our new century? Some feel that true sport has been taken over by big business and by television executives and agents. But over the last 100 years, sport has become more than a popular pastime, it has become a passion. This book describes the events that took place on some of the "great sporting dates" of sporting history.

◄ Karine Ruby won a gold medal for snowboarding at the Nagano Winter Olympics in 1998.

Don Bradman

Bradman breaks all cricketing records

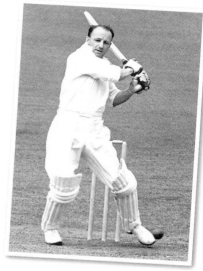

At the age of 21, the Australian, Donald Bradman, made cricketing history during the third test against England. He went in to bat when Australia were 2 runs for 1 wicket, and completed 100 runs before lunch. Batting all day, Bradman reached the huge total of 309 not out. He was at the wicket for 5 hours, 50 minutes. He broke all test match records with his amazing performance. The previous highest scorer was RE Forster, who made 289 runs in Sydney in 1904.

During the 1930 test match series, Bradman made a total of 703 runs. He was known for the ease and efficiency with which he achieved everything he wanted to do on the cricket pitch.

▲ Don Bradman in a test match at Trent Bridge

▲ Don Bradman batting during his record-breaking innings at Lords in 1930

In 1932, Douglas Jardine, the England captain, worked out a technique to unsettle the great Australian batsman. He got the bowlers to aim short balls at Bradman's ribs. This type of bowling became known as "bodyline" and is a **tactic** still in use today.

The plan worked well with some lesser batsmen, but not with Bradman. He went on to score many more runs for his country.

Len Hutton

On 23rd August 1938, the English batsman Len Hutton broke the world record for the highest number of runs ever scored in test match cricket. The record stood for 21 years.

Hutton breaks world record

▲ Len Hutton at the Oval –
Who dropped that catch?

Hutton, a Yorkshire player, was the first **professional** cricketer to captain the England side – and he never lost a **series**! His team won and **retained** the Ashes in the tough match against Australia in 1938. On that great day in August, at the Oval ground in South London, Len Hutton was at the **crease** throughout eight sessions.

He batted for 13 hours, 17 minutes to reach the amazing score of 364! England's total score was 903 runs for 7 wickets. Australia's wickets fell fast and they lost by an **innings** and 579 runs, which was one of their worst-ever defeats.

Len started playing cricket as a youngster, and in 1933, at the age of 17, he was invited to play for Yorkshire. He joined the England side in 1937. He often batted slowly, building up his score and making sure nobody got him out.

Sir Len Hutton was given his knighthood in 1956. He died in 1990.

The Matthews final

◀ The young Stanley Matthews, when he played for Stoke City

Stanley Matthews was called the "wizard of **dribble**" because of his ball skills. He was one of the greatest English footballers ever!

In May 1947, Stanley was transferred from Stoke City to Blackpool. He always wanted to be part of a team that won the FA Cup. However, Blackpool lost two finals – in 1948 and 1951.

"wizard of dribble"

▼ Matthews leading Blackpool to victory in the 1953 Cup Final

Blackpool faced Bolton Wanderers in the 1953 FA Cup Final. Bolton scored in the second minute of the game, and went on to lead 3 – 1. That's when Stanley Matthews took over! He ran down the **wing**, crossed the ball, and a team-mate scored. Then, with just three minutes to go, Matthews ran rings around the Bolton defence.

Blackpool gained a free kick and Mortesen scored, making the score three-all. He was the first player to score a **hat-trick** in an FA Cup Final. But from the next kick-off, Matthews took control. He ran past three defenders and placed a perfect pass for team-mate, Bill Perry to score the winning goal seconds before the final whistle. The match became know as the "The Matthews Final" because of his brilliant play that day.

He became Sir Stanley Matthews in 1965, and died in February 2000.

Muhammad Ali
– KING OF THE RING

Muhammad Ali once boasted that he was the most famous man in the world. He will be remembered as the greatest heavyweight boxer of all time. After winning an Olympic gold medal in Rome in 1960, Ali went on to win the world heavyweight championship on three separate occasions. This all-time boxing record is unlikely to be broken.

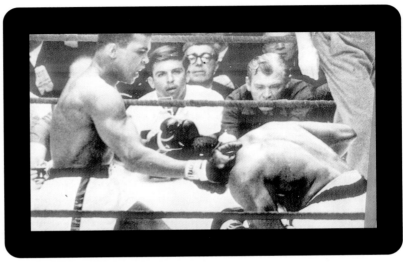

▲ Muhammad – "King of the Ring". His most famous saying was "I am the greatest".

▼ As Cassius Clay, the champion fought Liston again in 1965, and knocked him out in the first round. A few months later, Clay changed his name to Muhammad Ali.

Muhammad Ali enjoyed publicity and he liked to predict the round in which he would defeat opponents. He was often correct, and he become known as "the mouth". Most people thought he would lose to the hard-hitting heavyweight champion, Sonny Liston, when they met in Miami in 1964. He ran rings around Sonny Liston – and was declared the new world champion when Liston refused to carry on fighting in the second round.

Many people think boxing is a very dangerous sport because boxers get hit on the head too much.

Geoff Hurst

Although Association Football started in England in 1846, the England team have only won the World Cup once, in 1966. The competition was held in England that year, but just before it started the cup was stolen. It was found by a sniffer dog called Pickles.

Nobody expected England to do well. They had never got past the quarter-finals

A World Cup hat-trick

▲ At the 1966 World Cup, Hurst pulled off a hat-trick when he scored two goals in extra time.

before. The first game that England played was a 0 – 0 draw with Uruguay. Then the England team moved up a gear, and went on to beat Mexico, France, Argentina and Portugal, until they reached the final against West Germany.

England had well-known players in the squad but many people believed the Spurs goalscorer (striker), Jimmy Greaves, should have been picked, rather than Geoff Hurst of West Ham.

The West German team scored in the second minute of the game, but Geoff Hurst **equalized**. Thirteen minutes to go and Martin Peters, another West Ham player, scored. England 2, West Germany 1.

Surely England had won the World Cup! But with four minutes to go, Weber of West Germany snatched a dramatic equalizer.

Then, in extra time, Geoff Hurst scored two goals. He had scored the only World Cup Final **hat-trick**, and England became the 1966 World Champions.

▼ Bobby Moore takes the World Cup trophy from the Queen.

12

Brazil's third World Cup victory

In the 1970 World Cup Final in Mexico, the heat and altitude were a problem for some teams, including England, who were the winners of the previous World Cup in 1966. But Brazil's team always played entertaining, attacking football, and they beat Italy 4 – 1 in the final.

► Pelé celebrates scoring the first goal for Brazil in the 1970 World Cup Final against Italy, in Mexico.

The 1970 World Cup Final was Brazil's third victory – a World Cup record – so they were allowed to keep the original Jules Rimet trophy forever!

The Brazilian team was full of stars. The players to watch and admire were Pelé, Jairzinho, Gerson and Rivelino. The man of the match was Pelé, whose real name is Edson Arantes de Nascimento.

When Brazil scored their first goal, after just 18 minutes, everyone assumed they would win. But the Italian team had other ideas, and pressed for an equalizer. Then Italy made the mistake of becoming defensive, which allowed the Brazilian team to "play to its strengths". Although Pelé did not score directly, he created the opportunity for two of the goals, playing brilliantly as a team member and ensuring a victory for Brazil.

As a result of his dazzling displays on the field, Pelé was voted "Footballer of the Century".

The year before the World Cup, on 20th November, 1969, Pelé scored his thousandth goal. By the time he retired in 1977, he had scored 1257 goals in a truly dazzling career.

In the World Cup Final of 1994, Brazil became kings of the footballing world for the fourth time. Once again, they were up against Italy. By full-time neither team had scored, but Brazil finally beat Italy 3 – 2 in the penalty shoot-out.

Mark Spitz

Seven gold medals in one Olympic Games!

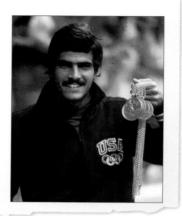

1972
MUNICH OLYMPICS

◀ Mark Spitz receiving his 5th gold medal in 1972

Mark Spitz's greatest moment came during the Munich Olympics in 1972. The 22-year-old American won seven gold medals for swimming. The previous record was held by the French fencer, Nedo Nuets, who won five gold medals in the 1920 Olympics.

Mark Spitz was born on 10th February 1950 in the USA. As soon as he could walk, Mark's parents encouraged him to swim. He swam in the sea every day and soon became the fastest swimmer in his area.

Mark competed in the Maccabiah Games in Israel in 1965, and won four gold medals. People realized he was destined to become the greatest swimmer of the modern world.

By 1972, Mark had set 23 world swimming records and 35 US records. However, in the Olympics in 1968, Mark had not performed as well as his trainers thought he might. But in the 1972 Olympics, he proved that he could win at the highest level. He gained his first gold in the 200-metre butterfly. He won that gold in style and set a new world record. The same evening he won a second gold for the US team – setting a new world record for the 400-metre free-style. Over the following days world records tumbled and Mark won more and more golds – another five!

After his 1972 success, Mark retired from swimming and starred in several films.

▲ Mark Spitz in the lead at the 1972 Olympics

Red Rum wins again

One of the most famous race horses in history was Red Rum.

Red Rum is "murder" spelt backwards. This horse certainly "murdered" the opposition! Red Rum had already won the Grand National twice, in 1973 and 1974. He came second in 1975 and again in 1976. The reason for Red Rum's success in the Grand National **steeplechase** was that he managed to avoid trouble. When horses tumbled, he kept clear. He seemed to always measure each fence before he jumped, and he could run with great power. After a race, Red Rum always appeared less tired than most horses. This was partly due to the care of his trainer, George McCain.

◀ Red Rum in training for the 1975 Grand National

The favourite to win the 1977 race was Andy Pandy, but he fell. Red Rum took the lead – chased by five other horses. He stepped up his pace, to win by 25 lengths.

Red Rum had made Grand National history by winning the event for a record third time!

▲ Red Rum, with his jockey Tommy Stack, heading for the finishing post and his third Grand National win!

Clare Francis sails in!

Sailing an ocean-going yacht single-handed requires great strength and courage. Clare Francis has the slight build of a dancer – she trained at the Royal Ballet School before taking an economics degree at London University – but that did not deter her from becoming a single-handed yachtswoman. Her first solo trip across the Atlantic took 37 days. She was the smallest person ever to have sailed across the Atlantic alone. Then she took part in the Round Britain Race, and made other epic solo voyages before deciding to enter the Transatlantic boat race.

**6TH JUNE 1977
SINGLE-HANDED TRANSATLANTIC RACE**

▼ Clare Francis testing the radio aboard her yacht, *Robertson's Golly*, in preparation for her single-handed race

The 1977 Royal Western Single-handed Transatlantic Race was the hardest ever, due to poor weather conditions. Clare had to battle against two violent gales, a storm and continuous fog. She also faced huge waves nearly 10 metres high. One morning, she woke up to find that she had sailed between two massive icebergs. She also had to overcome a stomach illness, as well as lack of sleep.

Deaths had never occurred in the Transatlantic Race before, but in 1977 several people were killed. There were more competitors than ever before. Of the 125 boats that started the race, only 73 finished. However, Clare Francis, in her 10-metre boat *Robertson's Golly*, managed to beat the women's record and complete the race 29 days after leaving Falmouth in England. She landed at Newport, Rhode Island in the USA on 6th June 1977.

Victory for *Australia II*
– THE AMERICA'S CUP

Until 1983, although the Australians had always been keen sailors, they had never managed to win the world's most prized yachting trophy, the America's Cup. The USA had won it 24 times in 24 attempts. They had never been beaten! Few people thought the Australians could beat the Americans, but the Australian, Alan Bond, and his team captain, Ben Lexcor, had other ideas.

Bond and Lexcor had designed a new **hull** for their boat, *Australia II*, that was

◀ *Australia II* had a revolutionary hull design.

better than the previous shape. They tried to keep the design a secret from the Americans.

The Americans were worried about how easily *Australia II* beat the opposition in the **heats**. They complained about the new design, which made them unpopular – even in the USA!

In September 1983, the race took place. The Americans won the first two races of the final series and everyone thought that the Australian team were beaten. However, *Australia II* won most of the following races, and finally took the America's Cup on 14th September. For the first time in 132 years, the Americans were beaten.

Since then, only New Zealand has ever taken the Cup from the Americans, and that was in 1995.

▲ The *Australia II* competed against the American yacht, *Liberty*.

17

Torvill and Dean

▲ Torvill and Dean with their winners' medals and bouquets of flowers.

◀ Torvill and Dean danced to the music of Ravel's *Bolero* in their winning routine.

Jayne Torvill worked in an insurance office before she met Christopher Dean, who was a constable in the Nottingham Police Force. They began ice-dancing together, developing their technique and routines.

After a great deal of hard work and practice, they competed in the 1980 Winter Olympics, finishing fifth. Encouraged by their performance at the Olympics, they went on to win three ice-dancing championships over the next three years.

On 14th February 1984, they competed at the Winter Olympics in Sarejevo,

Yugoslavia (now Bosnia). All nine judges gave the British skaters the maximum six marks for artistic impression. It was the first time nine perfect sixes had ever been awarded – a record that still stands.

Torvill and Dean became more famous than any other ice-skating champions before them. Now, they are the best ice-dancing partnership ever known. In 1984, they gave up competitions and turned **professional**, touring the world with their ice-dance shows.

Martina Navratilova

Martina Navratilova is the most successful woman tennis star ever known. The 2000 World Number One, Martina Hingis, is named after her!

TENNIS

7TH JULY 1990
WIIMBLEDON, UK

A record 9th Wimbledon victory

In 1983 and 1984, Martina Navratilova won more prize money than any other sports star. She has won all the grand slams – Wimbledon, the US Open, the French and the Australian Open tournaments.

Martina has won Wimbledon nine times. Her first victory was against the American Chris Evert. She went on to beat Chris in four other Wimbledon finals, although Chris was the champion herself three times.

In 1990, at the age of 33, Martina beat the younger Zina Garrison 6 – 4, 6 – 1. Zina Garrison was outplayed, as Martina won her ninth singles final before retiring. She now holds the record for the most Wimbledon victories by a lady champion.

Martina was born in 1957, in Czechoslovakia, and started to play tennis at the age of three. Her grandmother was also a very good tennis player. Martina has now become an American citizen. Her record now stands at 56 Grand Slam titles, 167 singles titles and 165 doubles titles. She came out of retirement in June 2000 to compete in yet more doubles matches.

▲ Martina with the Wimbledon trophy, having beaten Chris Evert in the final for a second time

◀ Martina at Wimbledon during her record-breaking 1990 season

Pete Sampras wins the US Open

When he was still quite young, Pete Sampras decided that he wanted to win a great tennis tournament. He prepared for tournaments by running, lifting weights and practising tennis.

At the age of 19, he entered the 1990 US Open tennis championships at Flushing Meadow, New York, and became the youngest person to win the title. He was **ranked** number 12, the lowest-ranked **seed** to become the winner since 1966.

During the championships, he remained cool while under pressure and he could **serve** the ball at 190 kph. His ground strokes were **fluent** and his **volleying** was perfect. He beat two former champions on his way to this title.

**17TH SEPTEMBER 1990
NEW YORK**

Pete Sampras ▶
hits a winning
return.

◀ Sampras holds Wimbledon trophy for the seventh time. It was his thirteenth Grand Slam title.

In the final, he faced André Agassi. Agassi's play was often unpredictable but he was determined to beat the young Sampras. However, Pete played some of his best tennis and won 6–4, 6–3, 6–2, which was a remarkable victory for such a young player.

Pete Sampras has gone on to win many more championships, including his record-breaking seventh win at Wimbledon, in June 2000.

Australia wins the Rugby World Cup

In the 1991 Rugby World Cup, Australia beat the famous All Blacks from New Zealand in an exciting semi-final. Having beaten the reigning champions, the Australian team were ready to take on England, but the English were going to be a strong challenge. They had just won the Five-Nations Championships by beating good opposition. Their new captain, Will Carling, led a strong side.

◀ David Campese, one of Australia's star players

This was only the second Rugby World Cup final. Everyone wanted a good, open game. The **groundsmen** had cut the grass very short to encourage a fast, running game.

By half-time, Australia had a 9 – 0 lead. In the second half, the England full-back, Jonathan Webb, scored with a **penalty**. As time ticked away, England became desperate. They had tried to beat Australia by feeding the ball to their forwards – but they suddenly changed **tactics** and threw the ball wide to the **wing**. The Australian defence coped with the pressure and went on to win 12 – 6, thanks to star players like Farr-Jones and Campese.

▲ Nick Farr-Jones wins a loose ball for Australia.

21

Sally Gunnell

Sally Gunnell, winning the Olympic gold, 1992

Star of the 1993 Athletics season

Sally demonstrating ▶ perfect coordination in the hurdles

Sally Gunnell is one of the greatest British athletes. She is best known as a sprinter and hurdler. She was an outstanding competitor in the 400-metre **hurdles** in the 1990s. By the time the 1993 season started, Sally had already won the Olympic gold medal for the 400-metre hurdles. She won this in Barcelona, Spain, in 1992.

During the 1993 season, Sally set a world record in the 400-metre hurdles. This was at the track-and-field world championships in Stuttgart, Germany. To win hurdle races, Sally had to practise hard to get her strides right in order to take each hurdle perfectly.

"she was a truly great champion!"

By the end of the 1993 season, Sally had broken 13 records. Eight of these records were in the 400-metre hurdles.

But 1993 was not Sally's final year of victory. She went on to win the 400-metre hurdles at the European Championships, the Commonwealth Games in Canada, and the Goodwill Games in Russia, all in 1994. Sally felt that the British fans, who cheered her on madly, gave her a terrific boost.

Jerry Rice touches down for a record

Jerry Lee Rice first played American football in 1985. He played for the San Francisco Forty-niners. He led them to a **hat-trick** of victories in 1989, 1990 and 1995.

He was a "wide-receiver", which is not a position that helps a player break records. His first-ever **touchdown** was made after he received a 25-yard pass by another legend, Joe Montana.

After four years of playing, Jerry made a team-record touchdown from 96 yards. He made another record when he scored three touchdowns against Denver in the Super Bowl.

In the first game of the 1994 season, Jerry faced the Los Angeles Raiders in a National League football game. He was determined to help his team win. He scored by making his 127th touchdown. This broke a record that had been held since the 1960s.

Jerry Rice has since gone on to break more records. By the end of the 1995 season, he had scored 156 touchdowns!

▲ Jerry Rice's record-breaking series of touchdowns made him a legend in American football history.

In the US, 1 yard = 0.9 metres

Brian Lara

◀ Brian Lara cracks a four while batting for the West Indies.

Brian Lara of the West Indies breaks record

Brian Lara reached 501 not-out for Warwickshire on 6th June 1994, and it gave him the world record for the highest number of runs in any county cricket match.

Just a few months before this victory, Brian Lara broke Sir Gary Sobers' test record by scoring 375 runs. This was on 18th April in Antigua in the West Indies.

Everyone interested in cricket knew the greatest batsmen's scores – Don Bradman (452 not out) and Len Hutton (364) were both well-known records. On this great day at Edgbaston cricket ground in Birmingham, Brian Lara broke the latest record. He also helped Warwickshire gain a great victory over County Durham.

The small, left-handed batsman is only the second man in history to hold both the highest test record and the highest number of runs at the same time.

When Brian Lara was only 20 years old, in 1990, he made his test debut against Pakistan. He scored 44 runs in his first test **innings**, which was a very good start. By 1994, his test average was 53.69 runs per innings!

Since his amazing victories, Brian Lara has gone on to make many more runs in test matches. Recently, the West Indies national side has slumped, and Lara's captaincy has been criticized. However, he should have many cricketing years ahead of him, and he may yet break more records!

Miguel Indurain

When Miguel Indurain first won the Tour de France in 1991, nobody guessed he would go on to win the race five times in a row.

Miguel Indurain, the cycling champion from Navarre, Spain, is the greatest cyclist in sporting history. Ever since the event began in 1903, nobody has achieved as much as Miguel. Three other cyclists have won the Tour de France five times – but none of them won five years in succession!

▼ Indurain heads for the finishing line.

JULY 1995 TOUR DE FRANCE

Spanish cyclist wins five-in-a-row!

Miguel was born on 16th July 1964. After he won the Spanish **Amateur** Cycling Championship, he turned **professional**. People soon realized that Miguel had the combination of strength and speed to race on the roads, and the stamina to manage the tricky mountain sections.

He first entered the Tour de France in 1985, when he was just 21, but he failed to finish. Soon, his form improved, and in 1990 he finished tenth. The following year he won the title. In 1992 he **retained** the title and won a time-trial stage, beating his nearest rival by three minutes.

Miguel won both the Tour de France and the Tour of Italy in 1992, and again in 1993! At the Atlanta Olympics in 1996,

▲ Indurain in the lead during the gruelling mountain section

Miguel won the gold medal in the individual time trial. He retired from professional racing in 1997.

Will Miguel Indurain's amazing record ever be beaten?

Tiger Woods

Tiger Woods is one of the greatest young golfers ever known. He began playing golf very early. At the age of six he played against Sam Snead, who had won the US Masters three times. Tiger lost by only one **stroke**.

Tiger won three **amateur** championships (1994 – 1996) before turning **professional**.

In 1997, at the age of 21, he won the US Masters, which was his first major title. In doing so, he broke a host of records:

- He went round the course using 270 strokes, beating the previous record of 271.
- He won by 12 strokes – which was the biggest-ever victory margin for that tournament.
- He was the youngest champion in 61 years.
- As his father is African and his mother is Thai, he was both the first African-American and the first Asian-American to win a major golfing championship.

▲ Tiger Woods with the US Open trophy. When Tiger was born in 1976 he was named Eldrick. His father nicknamed him "Tiger", after a soldier he had served with in the Vietnam war.

Since the 1997 victory, Tiger Woods has gone on to win two more major titles. He won the Professional Golfers' Association Championship in 1999, and the 100th US Open in 2000. He won the US Open by a 15-stroke margin, beating the existing record of 13 strokes, which was set back in 1862! To date, Tiger is the only player to hold all three major titles at the same time – the US Open, the US Professional Golfers' Association and the US Masters.

Karine Ruby

In February 1998, Karine Ruby, the French snowboarder, became the first woman ever to win an Olympic snowboarding gold medal.

Gold for Karine in the first Olympic snowboarding event

It was in the giant slalom event. She was the first victor on Mount Yakelitai at the Nagano Winter Olympics in Japan. Snowboarding had only just gained Olympic status that year.

The 21-year-old student had already won six consecutive World Cup events earlier in the year, including beating the reigning World Champion, Sandra Van Ent of the USA.

At the Nagano Olympics, the US women's team were expected to win, but the heavy snow and swirling winds caught riders by surprise. Karine's strongest challenge came from Heidi Renoth of Germany. Karine lost control at a gate on her crucial first run, but used her hands to recover her balance and finished in a record time.

By winning a gold, Karine had the honour of being the first winner of a new Olympic event. She will want to defend her gold medal at the next Winter Olympics in 2002, and as she says herself, she is still young enough to represent France at many more Winter Olympics.

◀ Karine, from Chamonix in France, started snowboarding at the age of 11, and in 1996 became World Champion, having won the World Cup title three times.

Khalid Khannouchi ...
FASTEST MARATHON

Khalid Khannouchi's first great success as a marathon runner came on 24th October 1999. The man from Morocco ran the Chicago marathon, in Illinois USA, in a record 2 hours, 5 minutes and 42 seconds. He took 23 seconds off the previous record, which was set by Ronaldo de Costa of Brazil on 20th September 1998.

That great moment in Chicago was not to be Khalid's last. In 2000 he went on to win the LaSalle Bank Chicago Marathon in a time of 2 hours, 7 minutes and 1 second. This replaced a previous record, set by David Morris, of 2 hours, 9 minutes and 32 seconds. Khalid had smashed the American record!

Not all of Khalid's battles have been on the running track. He had to fight a long battle off the field to become an American citizen. He eventually achieved this ambition on 2nd May 2000. He told reporters that gaining the citizenship was an emotional and special day in his life. The great marathon runner is now free to participate in the US Olympic marathon trials.

Although recently suffering from injuries, Khalid believes that his best is yet to come. His ambition is to run faster than his own marathon record of 2 hours, 5 minutes and 42 seconds.

▼ Khannouchi reaches the finishing line in the LaSalle Bank Chicago marathon.

Steve Redgrave wins 5th gold

Steve Redgrave gained a fifth gold medal at the Sydney Olympics, on 23rd September 2000.

◀ Steve Redgrave with the British coxless four team on their way to winning the gold

His team beat the Italians in the coxless four rowing championships.

To win his fifth gold medal, Steve Redgrave had to cope with illness in the form of diabetes and a bowel disease. He also had to maintain a training schedule of five hours a day, seven days a week. He trained hard and continuously for twenty years, to stay top of his sport and win the five medals.

Steve won his first gold in the Los Angeles Olympics in 1984 and he followed up this win with another gold in the Seoul Olympics in 1988. Many people felt that Steve's third gold, in Barcelona, was a fantastic sporting achievement. Winning a fourth gold in Atlanta made Steve a sporting hero in Britain as he and his team

▲ Steve Redgrave, Tim Foster, James Cracknell and Matthew Pinsent with their gold medals

were the only people to win a gold medal for Britain that year.

After winning his fourth gold, Steve said that if anyone saw him near a boat again they could shoot him! But had he retired? No! He came back to win his fifth gold in Australia in 2000.

Steve is the first athlete in the world to win five gold medals in an endurance event at five Olympics … an achievement that may never be beaten!

Jonathan Edwards
TRIPLE JUMPING

25TH SEPTEMBER 2000
SYDNEY, AUSTRALIA

Jonathan Edwards won an Olympic gold medal for triple jumping after years of trying. His determination and his religious beliefs helped him through the difficult times.

In 1995, Jonathan set an amazing world record of 18.29 metres in Gothenburg. After that his performance did not live up to expectation – but all that changed in Sydney!

Jonathan had always loved triple jumping. At the age of 21 he finished ninth in the world student games. The following year he travelled with the British team to the Seoul games, but failed to reach the finals. Four years later, Jonathan won the UK title and the world cup, but when he failed to qualify for the Barcelona Olympics in 1992, it was a great disappointment for him.

In 1995, Jonathan won the European cup with his amazing 18.29-metre jump. It is still the longest jump in history. That year he also broke the UK and world record. Everyone expected him to win gold in the Atlanta Olympics in 1996, but he only took the silver.

Jonathan almost pulled out of the 2000 Olympics in Sydney. Just a fortnight before, Jonathan's mother-in-law died. However, his wife encouraged him to go ahead, and thanks to his faith and the aid of his wife, family and supporters, he won the gold.

▲ Jonathan Edwards in the triple jump

Edwards performing brilliantly in a qualifying round ▶

30

Glossary

amateur A person who plays sport, or does some other activity, just for pleasure, without being paid.

crease In cricket, the crease is any of four lines near each wicket, marking the positions for the bowler or batsman.

dribble In football, to dribble is to run and turn and move the ball past opponents by skilful foot work.

equalize To level the score in a match by scoring a goal or point.

fluent Flowing and graceful movements

Grand National The major horse race of the year in Britain.

groundsmen People who look after the grass/pitch.

hat-trick Three successes in a row, such as three wickets taken with three successive balls in cricket, or three goals scored by the same player or team in football.

heats The first rounds of a sporting event where the winners qualify for the main competition.

hull The body or frame of a ship.

hurdles A running race with a series of low jumps on the track.

innings In cricket, a team that is batting rather than fielding is said to be having its innings.

penalty In some ball sports, if the opposition has done something against the rules, a penalty is awarded to your team.

professional A person who is paid money to play a sport, or some other activity.

rank To make a list of players, in order of success, judging them by their previous results.

retain To keep hold of something.

seed In tennis, a seed is a good player who is not matched against another good player in the early rounds of a tennis tournament. He or she is "seeded" so that there is more chance of the best players facing each other in the final rounds of a competition.

series In cricket, a series of several test matches between two countries.

serve To put the ball into play in tennis.

steeplechase A horse race with hedges and ditches to jump. It originally involved racing from village to village.

stroke In golf, a single shot or hit at the ball.

tactic A plan or technique to help a player or team to win.

touchdown In American football this means placing the ball over the line to secure points for your team.

volley In tennis, this means hitting the ball before it has bounced.

wing In football, either of the two sides of the pitch near the touchlines are called wings. A winger is a footballer who plays near the touchlines.

Index